Whi

Story by Mike Graf
Illustrations by Liz Alger

PM Extensions
Ruby

U.S. Edition © 2013 HMH Supplemental Publishers
10801 N. MoPac Expressway
Building #3
Austin, TX 78759
www.hmhsupplemental.com

Text © 2003 Cengage Learning Australia Pty Limited
Illustrations © 2003 Cengage Learning Australia Pty Limited
Originally published in Australia by Cengage Learning Australia

14   1957   17
23604

Text: Mike Graf
Illustrations: Liz Alger
Reprint: Siew Han Ong
Printed in China by 1010 Printing International Ltd

Whirlwind
ISBN 978 0 75 786893 1

Contents

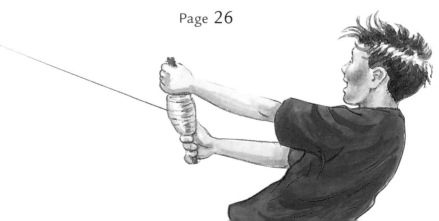

Chapter 1
Whirlwind

"**P**inebluff is a really pretty town," Dad said as he looked out over the small city. "We're lucky to live in such a great place."

"I know, Dad," Matt replied as he checked the string on *Whirlwind* – his brand new kite.

Dad stretched out the kite's tail. Then he picked up the kite and walked to the edge of the bluff.

Matt walked backward, and unrolled the line.

"That's as far as I can go," Dad called.

The wind was strong. The kite rustled as Dad held it high above his head. "Ready?" he called out.

"Ready," Matt replied.

Dad stretched his arms up high and thrust *Whirlwind* skyward. The diamond-shaped kite shot up.

As the kite rose, the tug increased. Matt leaned back and let the line out. He watched the kite lift higher and higher into the sky. *Whirlwind*'s long thin tail spun rapidly as it met the gusty winds above.

5

Slowly, Matt walked toward Dad at the bluff's edge. Soon, *Whirlwind* was way up in the sky.

"Better stay away from the edge," Dad warned. "I don't want that kite to pull you over."

Matt leaned back and held his ground. The kite pulled hard on the line.

Dad looked up and shielded his eyes against the dazzling sun. The blue sky was decorated with puffy white clouds. He gazed at the tiny kite jumping in the wind. "Let me know when you think it's high enough."

"It's pretty windy up here," cried Matt. He struggled to control the kite.

"Can you hold on?" Dad called back.

"Yes," Matt answered, "but *Whirlwind* wants to go higher." He took a few steps back, and held the line steady.

Dad pulled a steel rod from his backpack. It had a triangular loop at one end, and a corkscrew at the bottom.

"That's Buster's stake!" said Matt.

"I left the dog inside today, because there's a chance of storms later this evening," said Dad, "so I didn't have to tie him up. I thought we might be able to tie *Whirlwind* to this stake if the wind gets too strong."

Dad peered at the sky. *Whirlwind* was no more than a tiny dot. It danced around in the wind.

"It's going to take us a while to reel it in, huh, Dad?" Matt smiled.

"Doesn't matter," Dad answered. "We've got plenty of time."

Matt leaned further back. The kite was as high as the line would allow it to go, but it still wanted to go higher.

Dad looked at Matt. "Let's tie *Whirlwind* to the stake before we lose it."

Dad pushed the point of the stake into the ground and twisted it several times, until it was firmly planted. "All set," he said.

Matt pulled the kite line toward him, and knelt down next to the stake. He threaded the line through the loop and then tied a knot.

Dad shook the stake to make sure that it was secure. "That kite's not going anywhere," he said. He reached into his pack and pulled out a blanket. Then he spread the blanket on the ground and lay down.

Matt stretched out next to him.

Matt and Dad stared up at the sky. A cloud drifted in front of the sun, and for a moment it was shady. *Whirlwind* flicked about in the wind.

Dad yawned and shut his eyes. "There's nothing like a slow, lazy Sunday afternoon."

"Yeah," Matt agreed, as he shut his eyes.

Matt thought about his dad. He was happy to spend the day with him again. He'd been gone so much this spring. This had been one of the most active storm seasons in years, and Dad had been working very hard, chasing storms and tornadoes for the Weather Service. Matt imagined going with Dad on a storm-chase. He pictured being a crew member, reading the radar maps, and telling his father which roads to take to follow the tornado safely.

Soon, Matt started to doze off.

Chapter 2
Storm Clouds

A gust of wind whipped across the bluff. Matt opened his eyes and rubbed them, wondering how long he'd been asleep. He looked up at the sky. High above, he could see *Whirlwind* whipping about. Tall white clouds were gathering in the distance. "Dad, look!"

Dad opened his eyes and looked at the sky. "Hmmm … The weather forecast didn't call for all this until later," he said. "It shouldn't be a problem – those clouds are still quite far away. But we'd better keep an eye on them. We don't want to get caught in a storm."

"But it would be so cool!" said Matt. "We could chase the storm together!"

Dad laughed. "You shouldn't be too eager, Matt," he said. "Storm-chasing is exciting, but it can be pretty scary too, you know!"

"You must have seen some great storms," said Matt.

"I've seen a few," said Dad. "But I think the *best* one was the very first one I ever saw …

I was on my way home from school one day – I wasn't much older than you are now. A huge storm was blowing in. The clouds were dark gray, with a greenish-purple color underneath.

As I walked, it started hailing. I'll never forget how hard it hailed! First the hailstones were marble-sized, but before long they were bigger, and a few were as big as golf balls.

One huge hailstone smacked my arm. Another one glanced off the side of my head. I ran onto someone's porch, for shelter. But the hail broke through the awning on the porch.

I scrunched up against the door, hoping not to get pelted. I didn't even know who lived there, or if anyone was home. I just huddled as close as I could to that house and watched and listened to the crazy weather. It was hailing like mad. The hailstones were bouncing all over the place like ping-pong balls. And the wind was blowing wildly. Tree branches were shattered and blown about. I was stuck on that porch, soaking wet and cold, but too scared to move.

Where else could I have gone, anyway?

Then suddenly the hail stopped. It got eerily quiet. Slowly, I inched away from the door, expecting to be pelted by hailstones. The ground was completely white, and water was pouring from the roof. But the storm seemed to have moved on.

I walked off the porch and stepped into a deep puddle of ice. My tennis shoes were soaked in slush, and I was freezing. I remember thinking how weird it was – it had been really warm earlier that day. I wasn't even wearing a jacket!"

"I wish I could see a storm like that," Matt said.

"It was a beauty all right," said Dad. "I remember it so clearly – as if it were yesterday …

I looked up to see if the sky was clearing. A dark gray cloud covered the sky – but it was doing something I had never seen before. It was swirling, right above me! It was like a giant carousel, spinning in the sky. I looked around and realized that no one else was watching. I couldn't believe it was really happening!"

Plunk! A drop of rain splashed onto Dad's nose. He looked up. The sky was dark gray, and the sun had disappeared. A few more raindrops hit the ground.

Matt ignored the rain. "What happened next?" he asked.

Dad continued his story. *"I stood there, looking up at the swirling cloud ..."*

Ka-boom! Thunder rumbled in the distance. The rain fell harder.

Dad looked up at the sky. "We'd better head back to the truck," he said.

They jumped up off the ground, and Dad stuffed the blanket back into his pack. "I'll finish this story later," he said.

Matt remembered his kite. He looked up into the sky and saw *Whirlwind* thrashing about in the wind.

Lightning flashed. **Ka-boom!** Thunder rumbled, louder this time.

Matt grabbed the kite line, and fumbled at the knot on the stake.

Dad pulled Matt's arm away. "Don't!" he warned. "There's electricity in the air, and that's wet string attached to metal!"

Matt looked at Dad, "How are we going to get *Whirlwind* down?"

"I don't know, but we're not going to do it now," said Dad.

Ka-boom! Thunder rumbled, louder still.

Rain poured down from the dark gray clouds. Matt and Dad were getting soaked. They looked up. The clouds were starting to move in a circular motion.

"Unbelievable!" Dad exclaimed.

"What?" Matt asked.

Dad quickly looked all around. Their car was far down the trail, at least half a mile away. The trail was in open country, and was not a good place to run through in this type of weather. Behind them, at the top of the bluff, was a parking lot. Cars could drive up there, but Matt and Dad had hiked up from the opposite direction. Beyond the parking lot, a road wound its way off the back of the bluff, and down to the valley below.

Matt grabbed Dad's arm. "Look!" A small part of the cloud was spinning down from the base.

Dad watched the cloud for a moment. "That's going to be a big twister!" he gasped.

"Really?" Matt stared at the funnel-shaped cloud as it rotated and lowered to the ground. "We might get to go on a storm-chase after all!"

"But this time, it's the storm that's chasing *us*!" Dad hollered, as a gust of wind whipped across the bluff.

Chapter 3

Tornado

For a moment, Dad and Matt stared at the lengthening funnel cloud. Its sides vibrated as it snaked its way downward and moved toward the bluff. Sheets of rain whipped against Matt and Dad.

"It's getting too close!" Dad called out, bracing himself against the wind.

"Dad, look!" Matt cried. A short distance away, a dark cloud of dust was circling above the ground. The funnel cloud had touched down.

"That's a full-blown tornado!" Dad shouted.

The twister whipped around and around. Trees and bushes were yanked out of the ground and tossed into the air as the twister crept forward. The dust cloud at its base got thicker.

Dad grabbed Matt's arm. "Come on! We can't watch any more."

They took off, running away from the twister, toward the parking lot. Wind and rain blew against them, but they struggled forward as fast as they could.

They made it to the parking lot. A tree was ripped from the ground in front of them. Bushes whisked by. As they ran, powerful gusts of wind pummelled them and blew them sideways. Matt held on to Dad as they both tried to move forward. A loud roaring noise chased them. It sounded like a runaway train.

Matt turned to look back at the whirling tornado.

"Matt! Come on!" Dad pulled Matt along. "You're just like me – too curious for your own good!"

"Where can we go?" Matt asked.

"Follow me. Hurry up. We can make it."

They bolted across the parking lot and toward the road. Each step felt like slow motion, as gusts of wind and rain blew up against them.

Finally, they made it to the road. "Keep running!" Dad urged.

The tornado behind them got louder. A small whirlwind whipped past. More bushes and tree branches blew across the road.

"There!" Dad cried. "Straight ahead!"

They pushed forward, trying to get to the shelter of a tunnel in the road. As the wind whipped wildly behind them, they dived inside and scrambled to the center of the tunnel. They huddled against a dirt wall, shivering from the cold.

They looked out through the tunnel's opening. The tornado roared just a few hundred feet away. Instinctively, they covered their heads. They held still, waiting for the twister to hit.

Suddenly, the noise died down. The twister seemed further away. Dad and Matt opened their eyes and ...

In an instant, the noise was back. The twister was on the other side of the tunnel! The whipping winds and train-like roar returned. Matt and Dad watched the storm spin violently. This time, it moved down the highway and toward the distant hills. As it moved further away, it appeared to lift off the ground.

Chapter 4

The Greatest Show on Earth!

Once it seemed safe, Matt and Dad walked to the edge of the tunnel and peered out. The twister was becoming smaller. It snaked its way across the horizon as the sun began to peek out. Matt and Dad stood for a moment and watched in fascination.

"There's nothing more beautiful in nature – or more dangerous," Dad sighed. "Let's go and see what damage has been done."

"I hope *Whirlwind* is okay," said Matt.

They walked back through the tunnel. Bright sunshine reflected off the wet pavement. Steam rose up from the rain-soaked ground. Branches from trees and plants were on the road. Parts of the road's pavement had been ripped right out of the ground, leaving only the muddy dirt below.

Matt and Dad silently walked to the parking lot and looked toward the horizon. A massive cloud was heaped high in the sky. Most of the cloud was bright white, and piled up like gigantic pieces of cauliflower. But the base was a dark leaden gray. Everything that was underneath the cloud was hidden by veils of rain.

27

A lightning bolt lit up the center of the cloud. But there was no thunder this time. The cloud was too far away.

Dad put his arm around Matt, and stared at the giant cloud. "*That's* why I chase storms," he said. "Weather is the greatest show on earth!"

Matt looked at Dad. "I want to go with you next time you chase a storm."

"I knew you'd say that! One tornado, and you're hooked, just like I was," Dad laughed. "Come on, we'd better get going. I told Mom I'd have you back by now."

They walked across the parking lot toward the edge of the bluff, stepping over branches left by the tornado.

"Look!" Matt cried. The tie-post was still there, but the line lay flat on the ground.

They looked up at the sky for *Whirlwind*. But the kite was gone.

"I guess *Whirlwind* didn't make it," said Matt.

"But *we* did!" said Dad as he pulled the post out of the ground. "And I think that's good enough."

They headed down the trail toward the truck.

"That was a pretty powerful twister," Dad said. "It was one of the strongest I've ever seen."

"You never finished telling me about the first storm you ever saw," Matt said.

"Oh, yeah," Dad chuckled. "There was a tornado then too, but I never really got a good look at it. I heard later that it went through the outskirts of town and ripped off some roofs. I was so upset that I missed that! I guess that's what got me started. Now, any time there's a thunderstorm anywhere within a couple of hundred miles of home – well, you know what I'll be doing!"

"Yeah. Mom says that you'd rather chase storms than do anything else!"

"She's right," Dad said. "But look at what we got to see. This was by far the closest I've ever been to a twister." He looked straight at Matt. "And I never want to be that close again!"

"I can't wait to tell everyone at school what happened," Matt beamed.

"Yep – just like me." Dad smiled. "You'll be telling this story for the rest of your life."

Matt and Dad rounded a bend in the trail. The truck was still there, and it didn't look damaged. But the twister had ravaged the area by it. It looked as though a giant eggbeater had ripped through the countryside.

Matt pointed at the truck. "Look!" he said. "It's *Whirlwind*!"

The kite was smashed up against the car's window. Its tail had been ripped off, and the main body was in shreds. Matt lifted the kite off the truck and held it up. "Poor *Whirlwind*," he said.

"I'll get you another kite," said Dad.

"It's all right, Dad. Maybe from now on, I can chase real storms with you!"